A New True Book

EXPERIMENTS WITH CHEMISTRY

By Helen J. Challand

CHILDRENS PRESS ®

CHICAGO

High school chemistry class in Oruro, Bolivia

PHOTO CREDITS

© Cameramann International, Ltd.—Cover and all photographs

Historical Pictures Service—44 (5 photos)

© Fisher Scientific—21, 22, 24

John Forsberg—11

Len Meents—6, 8, 10 (right), 12, 13 (right), 14, 15, 17 (right), 19 (left)

Cover—High school chemistry class

Library of Congress Cataloging-in-Publication Data

Challand, Helen J.
    Chemistry.

    (A New true book)
    Includes index.
    Summary: A brief introduction to chemistry,
discussing atoms, molecules, the periodic chart,
chemical changes, and states of   matter. Includes
simple experiments.
    1. Chemistry—Juvenile literature. [1. Chemistry]
    I. Title.
QD35.C46   1988   540   88-11862
    ISBN 0-516- 01151-0

TABLE OF CONTENTS

BREAK THE WORLD APART

A sugar cube would have to be as big as New York City (above) before we could see the atoms in it.

The world is made of tiny particles called atoms. More than 103 different atoms. Atoms make up all the things that we see, smell, and touch.

You cannot see atoms unless many are packed together. A hundred million atoms in a row would be only an inch long.

WHAT DO ATOMS LOOK LIKE?

The center, or nucleus, of an atom is a dense ball made up of protons and neutrons. The rest of the atom is mostly empty space. In this space, flying around the nucleus, are particles called electrons.

The electrons move around paths, or energy levels, at different distances from the atom's nucleus. Only a

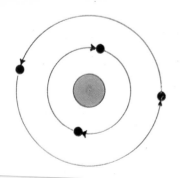
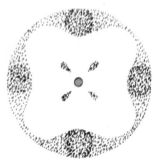

Scientists once compared the movement of electrons around the nucleus to the planets moving in orbit around the sun. Now they compare it to a cloud of particles moving around in space.

certain number of electrons can follow in the same path. Just two electrons can be in the first energy level around the nucleus. The next group has to fly around farther out. Eight electrons can be at this second level. The other levels can hold different numbers of electrons.

INSIDE HYDROGEN

Let's look inside the hydrogen (H) atom. Hydrogen is a gas that has no smell or color.

It has one proton in the nucleus and one electron outside the nucleus. But atoms are not stable unless two electrons are circling the nucleus.

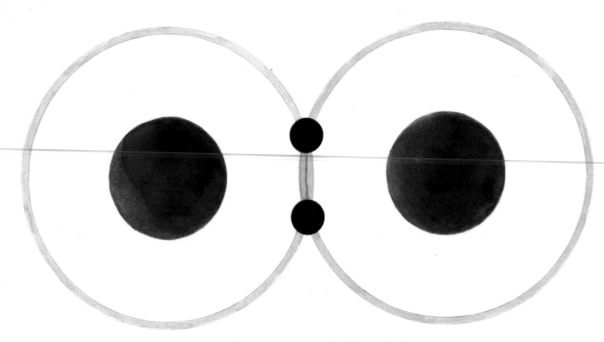

Two hydrogen atoms sharing electrons

Hydrogen atoms can become
stable by joining and
sharing electrons. Then
each nucleus has two
electrons. The joined atoms
are called a molecule,
which is written as H_2.

INSIDE OXYGEN

Oxygen (O) is a gas that has no color, smell, or taste. It is the most important atom on earth. Living things need oxygen for respiration.

Oxygen has 8 protons and 8 neutrons in its nucleus. It has 8 electrons, too. We know it can only have two electrons in the first energy level. That leaves 6 in the second

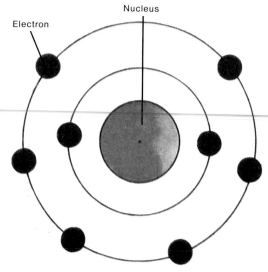

Electron

Nucleus

About 20 percent of our air is oxygen. Candles, coal, wood, and oil cannot burn without oxygen. An oxygen atom (right)

level. But atoms need 8 electrons in the second level. Oxygen needs 2 more electrons to be stable. When 2 oxygen atoms join to share electrons, an oxygen molecule (O_2) is formed.

WATER, WATER EVERYWHERE

Water covers three-fourths of the earth's surface. Humans cannot live without water. Plants need water to grow.

When two or more atoms join together they make a molecule. When two hydrogen atoms join one oxygen atom they make a molecule of water. Each hydrogen atom shares

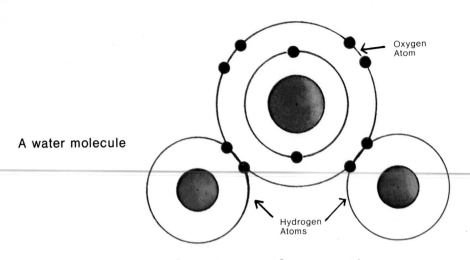

A water molecule

Oxygen Atom

Hydrogen Atoms

an electron from the oxygen atom, so they have two electrons in their first energy level. The oxygen atom needs two more electrons in its second level to reach eight. So the two hydrogen atoms each share their electron. The chemical recipe, or formula, for water is H_2O.

Diamond cutter (left) and diamonds (right)

HARDEST MATERIAL IN THE WORLD

A diamond is the hardest material in the world. It will scratch any other mineral or rock.

Diamonds are the purest form of carbon (C). Carbon is number 6 on the list

13

on page 21. Carbon has
6 protons, 6 neutrons, and
6 electrons. If there are
2 electrons in the first
energy level, the second
level must have 4. Since
that level needs 8 to be
stable, the atom must share
4 electrons. In diamonds,
carbon atoms share
electrons with each other.

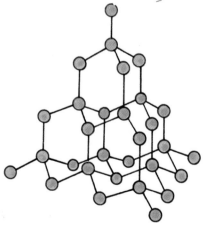

Carbon atoms forming a diamond

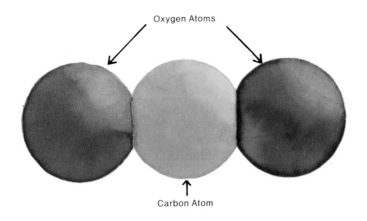

Oxygen Atoms

Carbon Atom

Atoms forming carbon dioxide

There is a gas called carbon dioxide that we exhale every minute. Human beings and other animals produce and release this gas. One carbon atom joins two oxygen atoms to make a molecule of carbon dioxide (formula CO_2).

HOW SWEET IT IS

We have been looking at only three different kinds of atoms. What sweet thing is made combining atoms of H and O and C? It is found in candy, pie, cookies, and cake. Industry gets this material from beet and cane plants. By now you know the answer, sugar.

Sugar is a big molecule. It takes 24 atoms to make it. Green plants know how to make sugar, but human beings cannot.

Sugar contains 6 carbon atoms, 12 hydrogen atoms, and 6 oxygen atoms. The formula for this sugar molecule is $C_6H_{12}O_6$.

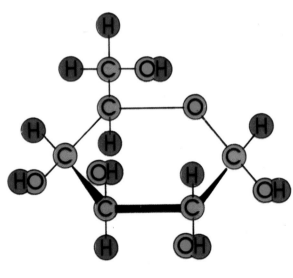

Atoms forming sugar

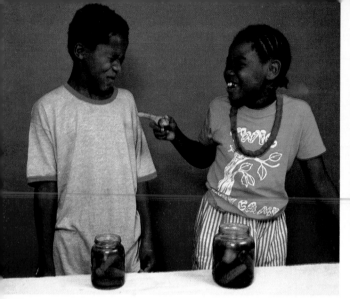

Vinegar is used in pickles (left) and in many salad dressings (right)

HOW SOUR IT IS

Now cut the recipe for sugar into three parts. We will use only 8 atoms instead of 24. Join 2 atoms of carbon and 2 of oxygen with 4 hydrogen atoms to make a sour

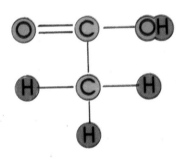

Atoms forming vinegar (above).

Bacteria (right) on a spoiled peach

material. You have eaten it
on salads and in pickles.
It is vinegar. Bacteria make
vinegar. They eat fruits
and make them spoil. The
waste left over is acetic
acid. Its formula is CH_3COOH.
Vinegar is made of this acid
mixed with water.

READING THE CHART

Chemists list atoms on what is called the Periodic Chart of the Elements. They use abbreviations for each element. O stands for oxygen, H is for hydrogen, and I is for iodine. If a letter is used once, then a second letter is needed. Ir stands for iridium. Iron is an element also. Since the chemists could not use I or Ir again, they

Periodic Chart of the Elements

Fisher Scientific

Cat. No. S45520

Main Table

Period	Element data
1	**H** 1 HYDROGEN 1.0079 — **He** 2 HELIUM 4.00260
2	**Li** 3 LITHIUM 6.941 · **Be** 4 BERYLLIUM 9.01218 · **B** 5 BORON 10.81 · **C** 6 CARBON 12.011 · **N** 7 NITROGEN 14.0067 · **O** 8 OXYGEN 15.9994 · **F** 9 FLUORINE 18.998403 · **Ne** 10 NEON 20.179
3	**Na** 11 SODIUM 22.98977 · **Mg** 12 MAGNESIUM 24.305 · **Al** 13 ALUMINUM 26.98154 · **Si** 14 SILICON 28.0855 · **P** 15 PHOSPHORUS 30.97376 · **S** 16 SULPHUR 32.06 · **Cl** 17 CHLORINE 35.453 · **Ar** 18 ARGON 39.948
4	**K** 19 POTASSIUM 39.0983 · **Ca** 20 CALCIUM 40.08 · **Sc** 21 SCANDIUM 44.9559 · **Ti** 22 TITANIUM 47.90 · **V** 23 VANADIUM 50.9414 · **Cr** 24 CHROMIUM 51.996 · **Mn** 25 MANGANESE 54.9380 · **Fe** 26 IRON 55.847 · **Co** 27 COBALT 58.9332 · **Ni** 28 NICKEL 58.70 · **Cu** 29 COPPER 63.546 · **Zn** 30 ZINC 65.38 · **Ga** 31 GALLIUM 69.72 · **Ge** 32 GERMANIUM 72.59 · **As** 33 ARSENIC 74.9216 · **Se** 34 SELENIUM 78.96 · **Br** 35 BROMINE 79.904 · **Kr** 36 KRYPTON 83.80
5	**Rb** 37 RUBIDIUM 85.4678 · **Sr** 38 STRONTIUM 87.62 · **Y** 39 YTTRIUM 88.9059 · **Zr** 40 ZIRCONIUM 91.22 · **Nb** 41 NIOBIUM 92.9064 · **Mo** 42 MOLYBDENUM 95.94 · **Tc** 43 TECHNETIUM (97) · **Ru** 44 RUTHENIUM 101.07 · **Rh** 45 RHODIUM 102.9055 · **Pd** 46 PALLADIUM 106.4 · **Ag** 47 SILVER 107.868 · **Cd** 48 CADMIUM 112.41 · **In** 49 INDIUM 114.82 · **Sn** 50 TIN 118.69 · **Sb** 51 ANTIMONY 121.75 · **Te** 52 TELLURIUM 127.60 · **I** 53 IODINE 126.9045 · **Xe** 54 XENON 131.30
6	**Cs** 55 CESIUM 132.9054 · **Ba** 56 BARIUM 137.33 · ***La** 57 LANTHANUM 138.9055 · **Hf** 72 HAFNIUM 178.49 · **Ta** 73 TANTALUM 180.9479 · **W** 74 TUNGSTEN 183.85 · **Re** 75 RHENIUM 186.207 · **Os** 76 OSMIUM 190.2 · **Ir** 77 IRIDIUM 192.22 · **Pt** 78 PLATINUM 195.09 · **Au** 79 GOLD 196.9665 · **Hg** 80 MERCURY 200.59 · **Tl** 81 THALLIUM 204.37 · **Pb** 82 LEAD 207.2 · **Bi** 83 BISMUTH 208.9804 · **Po** 84 POLONIUM (209) · **At** 85 ASTATINE (210) · **Rn** 86 RADON (222)
7	**Fr** 87 FRANCIUM (223) · **Ra** 88 RADIUM 226.0254 · ****Ac** 89 ACTINIUM (227) · **Unq** 104 UNNILQUADIUM (261) · **Unp** 105 UNNILPENTIUM (262) · **Unh** 106 UNNILHEXIUM (263) · **Uns** 107 UNNILSEPTIUM (262)

*Lanthanide Series

Ce 58 CERIUM 140.12 · **Pr** 59 PRASEODYMIUM 140.9077 · **Nd** 60 NEODYMIUM 144.24 · **Pm** 61 PROMETHIUM (147) · **Sm** 62 SAMARIUM 150.4 · **Eu** 63 EUROPIUM 151.96 · **Gd** 64 GADOLINIUM 157.25 · **Tb** 65 TERBIUM 158.9254 · **Dy** 66 DYSPROSIUM 162.50 · **Ho** 67 HOLMIUM 164.9304 · **Er** 68 ERBIUM 167.26 · **Tm** 69 THULIUM 168.9342 · **Yb** 70 YTTERBIUM 173.04 · **Lu** 71 LUTECIUM 174.97

**Actinide Series

Th 90 THORIUM 232.0381 · **Pa** 91 PROTACTINIUM 231.0359 · **U** 92 URANIUM 238.029 · **Np** 93 NEPTUNIUM 237.0482 · **Pu** 94 PLUTONIUM (244) · **Am** 95 AMERICIUM (243) · **Cm** 96 CURIUM (247) · **Bk** 97 BERKELIUM (247) · **Cf** 98 CALIFORNIUM (251) · **Es** 99 EINSTEINIUM (254) · **Fm** 100 FERMIUM (257) · **Md** 101 MENDELEVIUM (258) · **No** 102 NOBELIUM (259) · **Lr** 103 LAWRENCIUM (260)

Group header designations
New IUPAC: 1, 2, 13, 14, 15, 16, 17, 18
Former IUPAC: IA, IIA, IIIA, IVA, VA, VIA, VIIA, VIIIA, IB, IIB, IIIB, IVB, VB, VIB, VIIB, VIIIB
New Chemical Abstract Service: 3d–12d, etc.
Former Chemical Abstract Service: IIIB, IVB, VB, VIB, VIIB, VIIIB, IB, IIB, IIIA, IVA, VA, VIA, VIIA, 0

Legend
- ● New IUPAC
- ■ Former IUPAC
- ◆ New Chemical Abstract Service
- ★ Former Chemical Abstract Service

THE SYMBOL. Shown in the middle of each block directly below the name of the element. The color used indicates the physical state of the element under ordinary conditions: black for solids, green for liquids and blue for gases.

THE ATOMIC WEIGHT. Directly below the symbol for each element the atomic weight is shown in black. The weights are taken from the official Report on Atomic Weights C.A.J. Chem. Soc. 84, 4961 (1976). For elements not listed in the Report the mass number of the longest lived isotope is shown in brackets.

THE ATOMIC NUMBER. Shown in red in the upper left hand corner.

ELECTRONIC CONFIGURATION. Shown at the upper right as a group of black numerals. When read downward they indicate the number of electrons normally found in successive energy levels.

EDUCATIONAL MATERIALS DIVISION
4901 W. LeMoyne St.
Chicago, IL 60651
(312) 378-7770

©Copyright 1985

list iron as Fe after the
Latin name for iron, *ferrum*.

Each element is given a
number. The number of
protons or electrons in an
atom tells us its number
on the chart. The number
of electrons in each energy
level is written on one
side of each element. Look
for number 2 on the chart.
He or helium is a gas.
Notice that it has two
electrons. That is just
right to make it stable and

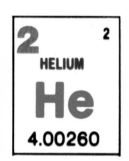

A balloon filled with helium gas (left) rises. Table salt (right)

not combine with another atom. This makes a fairly safe gas to use in balloons that float.

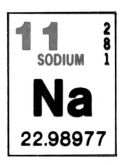

Table salt is made of two elements—sodium and chlorine. The symbol for sodium is Na. The symbol for chlorine is Cl. Their numbers are 11 and 17 on

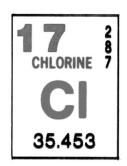

the chart. The number of electrons in the energy levels for sodium are two, eight, and one. The number of electrons in the levels for chlorine are two, eight, and seven. Since elements need at least eight electrons in the third level, you can see why these two elements combine easily.

Table salt is written as NaCl.

Most elements are grouped as metals or nonmetals. Metals usually have a shiny

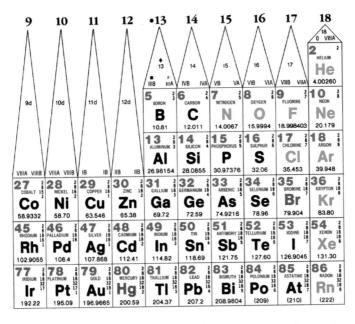

look. They will conduct
heat and electricity.
Gold (Au), copper (Cu),
silver (Ag), mercury (Hg),
and tin (Sn) are metals.
Some of the nonmetal
elements are carbon (C),
sulfur (S), fluorine (F),
and nitrogen (N). Can you
find them on the chart?

PLAY IT SAFE

Now you are ready to experiment with atoms and molecules. First a word of caution. Never put two materials together unless you know what they will do. Some materials will catch on fire. Some things will explode. Others will form an acid that will burn your skin. Still others make a gas that will burn your eyes or nose. Never touch, smell, or taste any chemical that is not safe. Experiment only with chemicals that your teacher, mother, or father say are safe to use.

POP A CORK*

Find a cork that fits into a bottle. Pour a cup of vinegar into the bottle. Put a tablespoon of baking soda on a small piece of tissue paper. Gather up the corners and tie it with a piece of string or thread. Drop this bundle into the bottle. Quickly cork the bottle. Do not push the cork down too tightly. Shake the bottle once or twice. Stand away from the bottle and watch what happens. A chemical change takes place. A gas, carbon dioxide, is given off.

* Ask an adult to help you with this experiment

A FEAST FOR YEAST

Divide a package of dry yeast in half and place each half in a plastic cup. Pour half a cup of warm water into each cup. Add one tablespoon of sugar to one cup. Watch what happens. Yeast is a plant that cannot make its own food. It feeds on sugar, breaking it down into carbon dioxide and alcohol. The alcohol smells like bread baking. You can see the bubbles the carbon dioxide gas makes in the water. What happened to the cup without any sugar?

ADDING OXYGEN

When you add 2 plus 2 you get a different number—4. Let's add two chemicals together and see what we can get. Soak a ball of steel wool with water. Put it into a covered glass jar. After a few days the wool becomes a brownish orange. This is rust, or iron oxide. Steel is made of iron. This is what happened during the chemical change: Two atoms of iron joined with three atoms of oxygen from the air. The formula is Fe_2O_3.

SUBTRACTING OXYGEN

Let us try to free up some oxygen in an experiment.

Buy a three percent solution of hydrogen peroxide for this experiment.

The formula for hydrogen peroxide is H_2O_2. It has one more atom of O joined to its molecule than does water, or H_2O. You can get this material to give up that extra O and make water.

Place some rusty nails in a metal can. Pour in hydrogen peroxide to cover them. Notice the bubbles coming up to the surface of the liquid. These bubbles are oxygen.

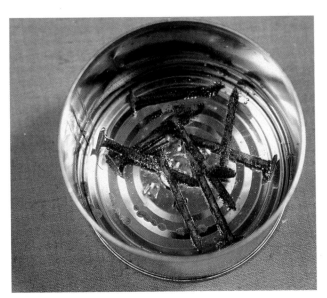

NOT TOO HOT TO HANDLE*

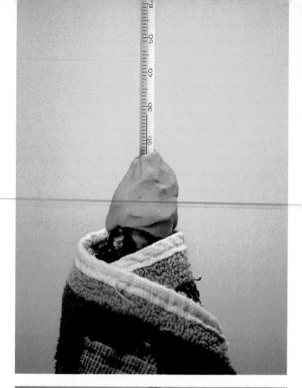

You will need a soda bottle, thermometer, ball of modeling clay, steel wool, and towel for this experiment. Wet the ball of steel wool and push it into the bottle. Push a thermometer half-way through the ball of clay. Lower the bulb of the thermometer into the neck of the bottle. Press the clay around the opening to make it airtight. Now wrap a towel around the outside of the bottle. Record the temperature at the beginning. After 15 minutes take another reading. Every half hour remove the clay and let in fresh air.

The wet steel wool takes oxygen out of the air. Oxygen combines with iron to make rust. Does this chemical change give off heat? Take off the towel and touch the bottle. It made the temperature rise, but it is not too hot to handle. Many chemical changes cause heat but often too little to feel it.

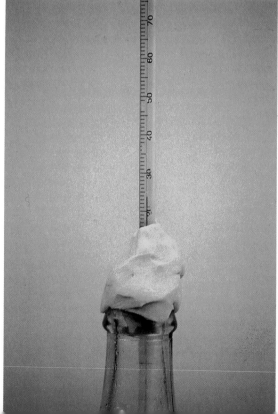

* Ask an adult to help you with this experiment

1 + 1 = 2 ?

For this experiment you will need two measuring cups—one that holds one cup and one that holds two cups.

Pour one cup of water into the larger measuring cup. Add a second cup of water. Does the liquid measure exactly two cups? Will this always be true?

Try two different liquids. Pour one cup of water and one cup of rubbing alcohol into the larger measuring cup. Do you still have two cups of liquid?

Molecules do not fit tightly together. There are spaces between them. Water

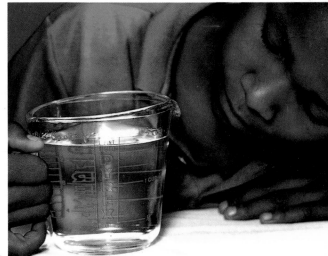

molecules fill in the spaces around the molecules of alcohol. Since there is now less space, you have less than two cups of liquid.

We can use big objects to see how this happens. Measure a cup of marbles or mothballs. Pour them into a mixing bowl. Add a cup of small seeds—peas or rice will do. Mix well. Now pour this mixture into the two-cup measuring jar. Did the two cups of these objects make a full two cups? This is what happened to the water and alcohol. You have just proved that 1 plus 1 does not always equal 2.

MOLECULES STICK TOGETHER

Fill a small drinking glass to the brim with water, but do not spill any water. Do you think any more water will fit in the glass? Predict how many more drops it will hold—10, 100, or more. Did you know there are billions of molecules in one drop of water?

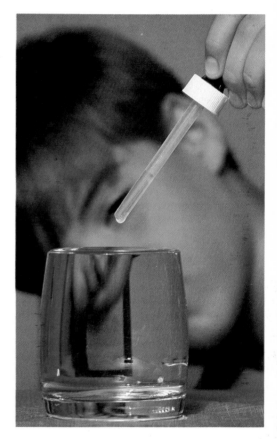

Use an eyedropper to count the number of drops of water that you add to the glass. Be sure the top of the glass is at eye level when you are looking at it. Can you see how the water piles up? Water molecules stick together. This stickiness is called cohesion.

Will molecules of oil stick together as well? Try this same experiment with cooking oil. Does oil act the same way as the water did?

Stir a few drops of dish-
washing detergent into a jar
of water. Fill a glass to
the brim with this soapy
water. Keep adding drops
until the glass overflows. Does
the soapy water make a bigger
or smaller pile on top than
the clear water or the oil?
Molecules of detergent get
between the molecules of water.
This keeps the water from
sticking together.

STATES OF MATTER

All the material on earth is in three states—solid, liquid, or gas. Molecules in a gas are spread apart. They move very fast. A glass may look like it is empty, but it is not. It is filled with air or gas. Gas has no size or shape.

You can push molecules of a gas closer together. Inflate a balloon part way. Squeeze it. It is soft because you have not put

too many molecules in it.
Inflate it up all the way. It
is so full that if you
squeeze too hard it will
break. Open up the neck of
a blown-up balloon and let
the gas out. It rushes out
so fast you can hear the
air move.

A liquid has size but no
shape. Fill a measuring
cup with water. Pour it
into a cake pan. You still
have a full cup of liquid,
but it is now spread out.
Syrup, milk, and oil are
liquids. They take the
shape of the container

they are in. Many liquids can be changed into a gas by heating. They can be made into a solid by lowering the temperature.

A solid has both size and shape. Things such as butter, foam rubber, and wool are soft solids. Steel, lumber, coal, and dry ice are hard solids.

Butter (left) is a soft solid.
Lumber (right) is a hard solid.

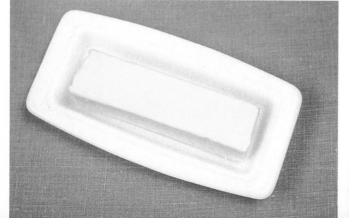

SMELLING MOLECULES IN A GAS

Spray some air freshener at one end of a room. Have a friend stand at the other end. How long does it take for the smell to get to her or him? You cannot see the molecules of the scent moving through the air, but you can prove that they do travel. They finally get close enough to smell. Even when the air is very still the molecules are always on the move.

SEEING MOLECULES IN A LIQUID

Fill a drinking glass with cold water. Put one drop of food coloring into it. Do not stir the water. Watch the color moving around in the water. How long does it take for all the water to be the same color? Try it now with a glass of hot water. Which water molecules move faster?

SOLID TO A LIQUID TO A GAS

Place an ice cube in a pan. Set it in the sun. Ice is solid water. Soon the ice becomes a liquid. Leave it in the sun until the water is gone. The liquid goes into the air. It is now a gas called water vapor. Can you guess when water goes from a gas to a liquid to a solid? It happens outside during the winter. The clouds are full of water vapor, which falls as a liquid. If the temperature is at freezing—around 32 degrees F.— the water turns to ice or sleet, a solid.

SOLID TO A GAS

Many solids turn into a liquid and then into a gas. This takes energy, usually in the form of heat. A few solids skip the liquid state.

Leave a mothball in an open dish for several weeks. Watch how it gets smaller. Does it melt like an ice cube?

Hold a mothball or a bar of scented soap near your nose. Can you smell it? Molecules leave the solids and go into the air. When we breathe the molecules we know that they are there.

FEELING MOLECULES IN A SOLID*

Set a metal spoon in a cup of very hot water. Hold the handle. Soon you will feel the heat in the spoon above the level of the water. Heat causes molecules to move faster. The molecules in the part of the spoon in the water bump into the ones above. As the molecules in the handle move faster you will feel the handle get warm.

* Ask an adult to help you with this experiment

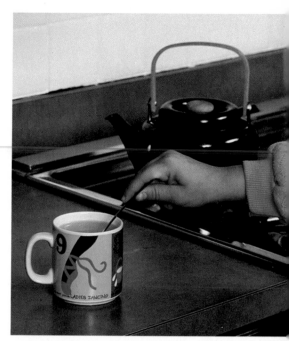

MIXING A CHEMICAL SOUP

You make a mixture by putting two or more materials together. They can be taken apart again. A new material is not made. No heat or energy is given off when you make a mixture.

Put these things in a bowl— pieces of rubber from a balloon, wood shavings, sugar, pebbles, sand, and iron filings. Cover with water and stir well. You have a mixture if you can get each one away from the others.

What things can you pick out with your fingers? Slowly pour off the water and save it. The sand and iron filings will be left in the bowl. How would you get the iron away from the sand? Try a magnet.

What happened to the sugar? You cannot see the molecules in the water, but they are there. Put the water in a cake pan. Set it in the sun or a warm place for several days.

You should end up with six piles of materials. The water went into the air, so you lost the seventh pile of chemicals.

THE END OF THE BEGINNING

Antoine Lavoisier, the "father of modern chemistry"

Robert Boyle

Albert Einstein

Niels Bohr

Ernest Rutherford

You have only begun to learn about chemistry. Read other books about atoms and molecules. Try more experiments. Look in an encyclopedia to learn about famous scientists. Read about Dmitry Mendeleyev, Ernest Rutherford, Albert Einstein, Niels Bohr,

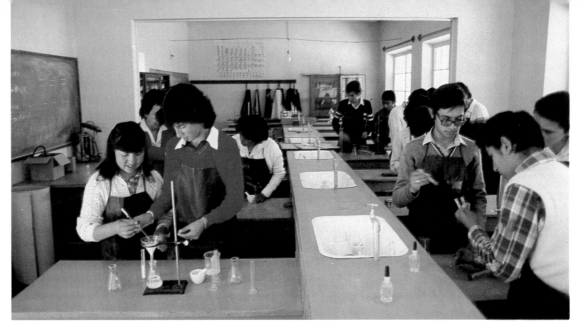

and Robert Boyle. Do not
forget Antoine Lavoisier.
He was called the father
of modern chemistry.
He lived over two hundred
years ago. Someday you
may want to become a
chemist. It is exciting
and fun to work with
atoms and molecules.

WORDS YOU SHOULD KNOW

atom(AT • um) — the smallest possible piece of a chemical element that can exist as that element

carbon(KAR • bun) — one of the earliest-known elements; exists in a pure state as diamond, in impure state as charcoal

chlorine(klor • EEN) — an element that is a strong-smelling gas; used in disinfectants, explosives, medicines

cohesion(ko • HEE • zhun) — the act or power of sticking together

diamond(DIE • a • mund) — one of the hardest known substances; made of nearly pure carbon

electrons(ih • LECK • trahnz) — tiny particles that move around the nucleus of an atom

element(EL • ih • mint) — the simplest form of each substance; the basic form of all material in the universe

exhale(ex • HAIL) — to breathe out

formula(FOR • myoo • la) — a statement showing how something is put together; a recipe

hydrogen(HYE • dra • jin) — the lightest element, an odorless and colorless gas

matter(MAT • er) — a solid, gaseous, or liquid substance

molecule(MAHL • ih • kyool) — the smallest piece of a substance able to exist alone without losing its original properties

neutron(NOO • trahn) — a particle found in the nucleus of an atom

nitrogen(NYE • tro • jin) — a gaseous element, colorless and odorless

nucleus(NOO • klee • yus) — the center of an atom, containing protons and neutrons

oxygen(OX • ih • jin) — a gaseous element, colorless and odorless

particle(PAHR • tih • kil) — a very small piece of matter

proton(PRO • tahn) — a particle found in the nucleus of an atom

respiration(ress • purr • AY • shun) — breathing; inhaling and exhaling; the burning of sugar by living cells

sodium(SO • dee • yum) — a silver-white metallic element found in many natural sources, such as plants, sea salt, rock salt

stable(STAY • bil) — lasting a long time without changing

INDEX

About the author

Helen Challand earned her M.A. and Ph.D. from Northwestern University. She currently is Chair of the Science Department at National College of Education and Coordinator of Undergraduate Studies for the college's West Suburban Campus.

An experienced classroom teacher and science consultant, Dr. Challand has worked on science projects for Scott, Foresman and Company, Rand McNally Publishers, Harper-Row Publishers, Encyclopaedia Britannica Films, Coronet Films, and Journal Films. She is associate editor for the Childrens Press Science Encyclopedia published by Childrens Press.